MILLIONAIRE MINDSET AND SUCCESS HABITS:

Break free from financial bondage and stand in your path to success and riches

DELMAR H. REYES

INTRODUCTION

In a world where financial freedom is both the aspiration and the elusive dream for many, **"Millionaire Mindset and Success Habits"** emerges as the guiding light to break free from the shackles of financial bondage. This compelling journey into the realms of prosperity is not just a blueprint for accumulating wealth, but a transformative odyssey that reshapes your thinking, propelling you onto the path of success and riches.

Picture this: a life where financial worries dissolve into opportunities, where success is not a distant mirage but a tangible reality waiting to be seized.

The title itself, a beacon of hope, promises not only to unlock the secrets of the millionaire mindset but also to cultivate success habits that are the cornerstone of lasting prosperity.

Embark on a voyage of self-discovery as you unravel the layers of your own potential.

"**Millionaire Mindset and Success Habits**" transcends mere financial strategies; it is a comprehensive guide that delves deep into the psychology of wealth creation. By understanding and adopting the mindset of those who have climbed the ladder of success, you pave the way for a seismic shift in your own financial trajectory.

This isn't just about amassing wealth; it's about creating a life of abundance, purpose, and significance. The book becomes a trusted companion, navigating you through the web of beliefs and behaviors that either propel individuals towards riches or keep them ensnared in the cycle of lack.

The narrative is not just informative; it is a call to action, challenging you to break free from the constraints that have held you back.

Imagine rewiring your thought patterns, aligning them with the principles that millionaires swear by. **"Millionaire Mindset and Success Habits"** is your passport to a world where financial worries are replaced by a confident stride towards your goals.

It doesn't offer a shortcut, but a proven roadmap that guides you through the labyrinth of challenges, towards the treasure trove of success. The allure of the title lies not only in its promise of financial liberation but in its emphasis on cultivating success habits. These habits, meticulously dissected and expounded upon, are the building blocks of a life steeped in achievement.

From the morning rituals that set the tone for a day of productivity to the bedtime practices that nurture a mindset of abundance, each habit is a stepping stone towards the pinnacle of success.

As you go into it, deeper and deeper, you encounter not only success stories that inspire but also the pitfalls that others have navigated. It's a reality check, a reminder that the journey to financial success is paved with challenges, setbacks, and resilience.

The narrative weaves together practical advice, psychological insights, and motivational anecdotes, creating a force that resonates with both the aspiring entrepreneur and the seasoned professional.

It's not about overnight success or get-rich-quick schemes; it's about instilling enduring habits that sustain prosperity. The book doesn't promise miracles; instead, it empowers you to become the architect of your own success story.

So, are you ready to shatter the chains that bind you to financial mediocrity?

Can you envision a life where success is not an exception but a habit? "Millionaire Mindset and Success Habits" beckons you to step into the realm of possibilities, to embrace a mindset that attracts abundance and to cultivate habits that propel you towards success and riches. .

Are you ready? Let's dive in!

UNLOCKING THE MILLIONAIRE MINDSET: A PARADIGM SHIFT

A millionaire mentality is focused with zeroing in on transforming yourself, beginning with your viewpoint, to achieve the objectives you've generally longed for accomplishing. Positive thinkers and imaginative visionaries make up millionaires.

To put it another way, wealthy people believe their big dreams will come true. Thus, abundance searchers ought to lay out grand objectives and not fear a strange area.

Having a millionaire mindset is equivalent to being rich intellectually and monetarily, seeing yourself in that extraordinary place of significance and influence.

A huge number are not simply fruitful financial specialists, they are enthusiastic about what they do and how they constructed their business.

This adoration for their work keeps them roused to continue onward, and to keep working on their organization.

You must spend time throughout your lifetime opening up your entire brain in order to become effective at the focused effort and hard work required to adopt a millionaire mindset. You need to drive yourself to go to places you have never thought for even a second to go. Assuming you are inventive, they foster the legitimate side.

10 Tips to Becoming a Millionaire

- Avoid obligation.
- Contribute early and reliably.
- Focus on investment funds.
- To achieve your objective more quickly, boost your income.
- Cut pointless costs.
- Keep your mogul objective up front.
- Work with an expert in investing.
- Peruse mogul books.
- Understand what you need and what you want.
- Set your strategy to repeat.

Rich individuals commonly put away their cash carefully, looking for proficient guidance when required. They comprehend that developing their abundance requires settling on informed venture choices.

They do not merely permit their funds to remain in savings accounts; all things being equal, they use it carefully through speculations.

Seven Core Rules for Creating Wealth These straightforward but potent guidelines can assist you in achieving your financial objectives. So, let's take a look at each rule and see how you can put them into practice in your life.

Rule 1:

There isn't a moment to spare

With regards to creating financial momentum, time is your most important resource. The previous you start, the additional time you need to develop your cash. Yet, regardless of whether you're beginning further down the road, just sit back and relax. The key is to begin now and be predictable.

Rule 2:

Saving forcefully matters.

To create financial wellbeing, you really want to forcefully save. Intend to save somewhere around 5% of your pay, and that's just the beginning if possible. Cut superfluous costs, and divert that cash towards your investment funds.

Practice saving regularly by setting up programmed moves from your financial records to your investment account. Like that, you will not need to superfluously spend.

Rule 3:

Resource allotment is the key

Resource allotment is the method involved with splitting your speculations between various resource classes like stocks, bonds, and land. It's vital to enhance your portfolio and equilibrium hazard and return.

Rule 4:

Feelings should be controlled

Feelings can prompt confounding choices, particularly with regards to effective money management. Dread and eagerness are two of the most well-known feelings that can make financial backers go with unfortunate choices.

Maintaining discipline and adhering to your investment plan is crucial.

Try not to allow feelings to hinder your drawn out objectives, never let that occur.

Rule 5:

Try not to pass up abundance insurance

Abundance security is in many cases ignored chasing after abundance creation. It's essential to safeguard your abundance through protection, home preparation, and resource security procedures. These crucial aspects of wealth management should not be overlooked.

Rule 6:

Develop yourself. Creating financial momentum isn't just about collecting cash. It's likewise about building yourself and making different kinds of revenue. Put resources into yourself through training, expertise building, and business. Making different floods of pay can assist you with accomplishing independence from the rat race and security.

UNDERSTANDING FINANCIAL FREEDOM: BREAKING THE CHAINS

Financial freedom is something beyond an idea; it is a significant condition of being that many try to accomplish. It includes breaking the chains of monetary imperatives, permitting people to carry on with life in their own specific manner. Understanding independence from the rat race isn't just about collecting abundance yet additionally about dealing with one's financial fate.

At its center, independence from the rat race is the capacity to settle on decisions without being impeded by monetary imperatives. It connotes freedom from the shackles of obligation, the pressure of living check to check, and the stress over how to cover fundamental costs.

Breaking these chains requires a major change in mentality and key activities to fabricate a strong monetary establishment.

To leave on the excursion of understanding independence from the rat race, one must initially survey what is going on. This includes investigating pay, costs, obligations, and resources. Making an unmistakable picture of where one stands monetarily gives the important beginning stage to planning a way to opportunity.

The foundation of breaking free monetarily is fostering a financial plan that lines up with both momentary requirements and long haul objectives.

A very much created financial plan fills in as a guide, directing people to distribute reserves carefully, save reliably, and contribute in a calculated way.

It engages them to assume command over their cash as opposed to being constrained by it.

Breaking the chains of monetary impediment likewise involves developing a reserve funds mentality.

This includes reliably saving a piece of pay for crises, open doors, and future objectives. The force of reserve funds lies in collecting assets as well as in making a security net that safeguards against unforeseen monetary difficulties.

Putting is a critical component in the excursion to independence from the rat race.

Instead of allowing cash to sit inactive, vital ventures can possibly develop abundance over the long haul. Grasping different venture vehicles, risk resilience, and long haul objectives are vital parts of compelling establishing a strong financial foundation procedures.

One more basic part of independence from the rat race is obligation to the board. Breaking free requires a proactive way to deal with decreasing and wiping out exorbitant interest obligations. This might include making an obligation reimbursement plan, rethinking terms, or looking for proficient counsel to explore complex monetary circumstances.

Building numerous floods of pay is a procedure utilized by the individuals who have effectively broken free monetarily.

Differentiating pay sources gives security and strength against monetary vulnerabilities. This could include investigating part time jobs, speculations, or enterprising endeavors.

Monetary training is a useful asset in the munitions stockpile of those looking to comprehend and accomplish independence from the rat race. It goes past customary tutoring and includes constant finding out about individual accounting, speculation methodologies, and monetary patterns. Information engages people to go with educated choices and explore the intricacies regarding the monetary scene.

Understanding independence from the rat race additionally requires tending to the mental parts of cash. This incorporates looking at convictions and perspectives towards riches, achievement, and overflow. Moving from a viewpoint that everything is limited to an overflow mentality makes the way for additional opportunities and open doors.

Breaking the chains of monetary limit and understanding independence from the rat race includes a blend of vital preparation, restrained monetary propensities, continuous schooling, and a change in mentality.

As people make purposeful strides towards independence from the rat race, they gain monetary freedom as well as the capacity to carry on with a daily existence lined up with their qualities and yearnings.

Here are steps that individuals can take to work towards breaking free from the cycle of poverty

- **Schooling and Expertise Advancement:**

Put resources into schooling and expertise advancement to upgrade employability.
Obtain abilities that are sought after in the gig market.

- **Monetary Education:**

Find out about individual accounting and planning.

Figure out the significance of saving and contributing for what's to come.

- **Business Open doors:**

Effectively look for business open doors that line up with abilities and interests.
Investigate work preparing projects or apprenticeships.

- **Business venture:**

Consider business ventures as a way to make pay.
Begin private ventures in view of abilities and interests.

- **Organizing and Coaching:**

Construct an organization of steady people who can give direction.

Look for coaches who have effectively defeated neediness.

CULTIVATING A SUCCESS MINDSET: REWIRING YOUR THOUGHTS

The human brain is a strong power, fit for molding our world in light of the examples of thought we develop. Developing a triumph mentality includes deliberately reworking our contemplations, convictions, and perspectives to cultivate a positive and strong point of view.

This change can possibly open new doors, upgrade by and large prosperity, and make ready for individual and expert achievement.

Understanding The Mind-set

A mindset is a bunch of convictions or mentalities that shape how people see and answer their general surroundings.

The division between a decent outlook and a development mentality, an idea presented by clinician Tune Dweck, is especially pertinent to developing achievement.

Fixed Mindset:

People with a decent outlook accept that their capacities and insight are static qualities. They might avoid difficulties, dreading disappointment as an impression of their innate capacities.

Growth Mindset:

On the other hand, those with a development outlook embrace difficulties as any open doors for development. They comprehend that work and steadiness can prompt improvement and achievement.

The Power of Positive Thinking

Positive thinking is an essential component of a triumph mentality. It includes zeroing in on arrangements as opposed to issues, seeing open doors in the midst of difficulties, and keeping a hopeful standpoint. Research proposes that positive reasoning can prompt superior pressure on the board, better well being results, and expanded versatility.

Strategies for Cultivating a Success Mindset

- **Self-Awareness:**

Start by becoming mindful of your ongoing idea designs.

Distinguish any self-restricting convictions that might be impeding your advancement.

- **Challenge Negative Thoughts:**

Effectively challenge negative considerations and supplant them with positive insistences.

Perceive the effect of self-chat on feelings and conduct.

- **Embrace Challenges:**

View difficulties as any open doors for learning and development.

Shift your viewpoint from keeping away from trouble to embracing it as a venturing stone to progress.

- **Continuous Learning:**

Develop an affection for learning and view mishaps as important illustrations.

Look for valuable open doors for individual and expert turn of events.

- **Set Realistic Goals:**

Lay out clear and attainable objectives.

Separate huge objectives into more modest, reasonable advances.

- **Celebrate Progress:**

Recognize and celebrate little triumphs en route.

Develop a mentality of appreciation for the excursion.

- **Surround Yourself with Positivity:**

Fabricate a strong organization of people who motivate and empower you.

Limit openness to cynicism in your current circumstance.

- **Visualize Success:**

Make a psychological picture of your ideal achievement. Use perception procedures to support positive results.

THE POWER OF VISUALIZATION: MANIFESTING WEALTH AND PROSPERITY

Visualization is the demonstration of shaping mental pictures to help one comprehend or accomplish specific objectives. An interaction includes our faculties, innovativeness, and creative mind. It permits us to guide our considerations to zero in on what makes the biggest difference to us and specifically take care of subtleties.

Visualization includes making clear mental pictures of explicit results or objectives. When applied to the domain of riches and flourishing, it implies intellectually encountering the overflow one tries to accomplish. This training takes advantage of the psyche mind, impacting insights and ways of behaving to line up with the imagined achievement.

At the center of visualization lies the pattern of good following good, an all inclusive rule proposing that like draws in like. As indicated by this regulation, the energy and considerations people transmit into the universe draw in comparative energies, at last forming their encounters.

Perception fills in as an engaged and deliberate utilization of the pattern of good following good, guiding one's contemplations toward the ideal monetary results.

Imagining results that you need can expand your certainty. "Seeing" yourself succeed assists you with accepting that it would be able, and will occur. Representation helps you "practice" achievement.

At the point when you envision each step of an occasion or movement working out in a good way, you prepare your brain and body to make those strides, all things considered.

As per this "all inclusive regulation", like draws in like. For example, assuming you center around sure considerations, positive things will happen to you. Also, assuming you center around the negative, terrible things will happen to you. This truly intends that, assuming you ponder abundance, odds are you will draw in abundance to your life.

At the core of showing abundance is the development of a positive mentality. Positive contemplations are accepted to radiate vibrations that resound with comparable energies in the universe, eventually drawing in relating encounters. By reliably keeping up with hopeful contemplations about monetary overflow, people open themselves to open doors that line up with their positive energy.

Practical Steps for Manifesting Wealth and prosperity

- **Clarify Financial Goals:**

Characterize explicit and attainable monetary objectives.

Separate bigger goals into significant stages.

- **Create a Vision Board:**

Order pictures and words addressing monetary objectives.

Viewable signs act as everyday updates and build up certain considerations.

- **Practice Gratitude:**

Develop appreciation for existing favors.

Appreciation enhances positive energy and draws in more overflow.

- **Affirmations and Visualization:**

Create positive confirmations connected with abundance.

Consolidate confirmations with striking perception to fortify conviction.

- **Release Resistance:**

Distinguish and deliver restricting convictions around cash.

Embrace a mentality of overflow without dread or uncertainty.

STRATEGIC GOAL SETTING: BLUEPRINT FOR SUCCESS

What is a general blueprint for achieving a goal?

A plan is a blueprint for objective accomplishment and it indicates the essential asset portion, timetables, assignments, and different activities. meaning of the reason that recognizes the association from others. A very much planned statement of purpose can upgrade representative inspiration and hierarchical execution

The Importance of Goal Setting

Goal setting is a useful asset that can assist you with keeping on track and persuaded as you pursue your desires.

At the point when you put forth clear and explicit objectives, you make a guide for your future, making it more straightforward to focus on your time and exertion.

Having objectives likewise gives an internal compass and motivation, and assists you with remaining fixed on what means quite a bit to you.

TIPS FOR SETTING SMART AND SUCCESSFUL GOALS

Smart goals are a well known and successful objective setting system that can assist you with defining objectives that are Explicit, Quantifiable, Reachable, Pertinent, and Time-bound.

- **Explicit:** Your objective ought to be clear and explicit so you know precisely everything you need to accomplish. A particular objective responds to the inquiries of who, what, where, when, and why.

- **Quantifiable**: Your objective ought to be quantifiable so you can keep tabs on your development and decide if you have accomplished your objective. A quantifiable objective incorporates explicit numbers or measurements that you can use to keep tabs on your development.

- **Reachable**: Your objective ought to be reachable, implying that it is reasonable and feasible given your ongoing assets and conditions. Feasible objectives challenge you, however they are likewise reachable with difficult work and commitment.

- **Pertinent:** Your objective ought to be important, implying that it lines up with your qualities, needs, and inspirations and that it seriously affects your life.

Constructing Your Blueprint for Success

- **Goal Identification:**

Investigate individual and expert desires.

Recognize short, medium, and long haul objectives.

- **SWOT Analysis:**

Evaluate Qualities, Shortcomings, Open doors, and Dangers. Influence qualities and amazing open doors while tending to shortcomings and dangers.

- **Actionable Steps:**

Foster a bit by bit intends to accomplish every objective. Characterize achievements and designated spots for progress assessment.

- **Time Management:**

Assign devoted time for objective related exercises. Offset momentary errands with long haul goals.

MASTERING TIME MANAGEMENT: MAXIMIZING PRODUCTIVITY

Time is our most precious currency. To master time management is to open the ways to unmatched efficiency and individual satisfaction. This extraordinary excursion isn't just about getting more undertakings into a day however about organizing time as one with our objectives and goals.

The Symphony of Time: Understanding the Composition

- **Conscious Time Awareness:**

Start by cultivating a significant consciousness of how time is spent. Recognize the fleeting assets accessible every day.

- **Prioritization:**

The foundation of successfully using time effectively, is prioritization. Recognize earnest and significant errands to carefully distribute energy.

- **Setting Clear Objectives:**

Obviously characterized goals act as the directing stars. Lay out present moment and long haul objectives to coordinate everyday activities.

- **Breaking Down Tasks:**

Overpowering undertakings become reasonable through discontinuity. Partition bigger undertakings into more modest, absorbable parts.

How can I Cultivate Time Management Habits?

- **Effective Planning:**

Engage in proactive planning.

Weekly, monthly, and yearly planners serve as navigational tools.

- **Eliminating Procrastination:**

Address the root causes of procrastination.

Break tasks into smaller steps to reduce intimidation.

- **Time Blocking:**

Allocate dedicated time blocks to specific activities. Enhance focus and minimize multitasking.

- **Intelligent Delegation:**

Recognize when to delegate tasks.

Empower others and free personal bandwidth.

- **Digital Tools:**

Integrate technology for streamlined workflows.

Calendar apps, task management tools, and productivity apps enhance efficiency.

- **Automation:**

Automate repetitive and time-consuming tasks.

Allows for increased focus on high-priority activities.

- **Digital Detox:**

Establish boundaries with technology.

Periodic digital detox promotes mindfulness and reduces distractions.

Steps to Navigating Time Challenges to making success.

- **Overcoming Decision Fatigue:**

Simplify decision-making processes.

Reduces mental fatigue and preserves cognitive resources.

- **Learning to Say No:**

Recognize personal limits and constraints.

Saying no is a powerful tool for preserving time and energy.

- **Adapting to Change:**

Cultivate flexibility in planning.

Adaptable schedules accommodate unexpected disruptions.

What are the Impact of Effective Time Management?

- **Enhanced Productivity:**

Accomplish more in less time.

Improved focus and efficiency amplify productivity.

- **Reduced Stress Levels:**

Efficient time management alleviates stress.

Clear schedules instill a sense of control.

- **Balancing Work and Life:**

Achieve a harmonious work-life balance. Quality time for personal pursuits and relationships.

How to Cultivate a Mindset of Productivity

- **Mindful Presence:**

Embrace mindfulness in daily activities.
Being fully present enhances the quality of work.

- **Continuous Learning:**

Learn from experiences and adapt strategies.
A growth mindset fuels ongoing improvement.

- **Celebrating Achievements:**

Acknowledge accomplishments along the way. Positive reinforcement fuels motivation.

INVESTING IN YOURSELF: EDUCATION AND PERSONAL GROWTH

One of the most significant speculations an individual can make is in themselves. This speculation rises above monetary portfolios; it envelops the enhancement of information, abilities, and self-awareness.

As the world develops at a remarkable speed, the significance of constantly putting resources into oneself becomes fundamental. This investigation digs into the meaning of such a venture and outlines significant stages toward encouraging self-improvement and

The Significance of Investing in Yourself

- **Continuous Adaptation:**

In a quickly impacting world, the capacity to adjust is a key part for progress.

Putting resources into oneself guarantees remaining applicable and dexterous in developing conditions.

- **Unleashing Potential:**

Each individual has undiscovered possibilities ready to be found.

Self-venture opens dormant gifts, making them ready for individual and expert satisfaction.

- **Empowerment and Confidence:**

Instruction and self-improvement engage people to explore difficulties.

Certainty blossoms as skills extend, making a positive criticism circle.

- **Enhanced Problem-Solving:**

A developed psyche is skilled at imaginative critical thinking. Putting resources into oneself improves decisive reasoning abilities fundamental for beating snags.

- **Lifelong Learning Mentality:**

A promise to self-speculation cultivates a mentality of deep rooted learning.

Embracing interest guarantees an improving excursion paying little heed to the mature or professional stage.

How can i Invest in myself?

- **Set Clear Goals:**

Characterize explicit, quantifiable, attainable, important, and time-bound (Brilliant) objectives.

Clearness in goals directs the choice of instructive pursuits and self-improvement exercises.

- **Prioritize Learning:**

Apportion committed time for learning attempts. Whether through proper schooling, studios, or independent review, steady learning is vital.

- **Read Widely and Diversely:**

Grow points of view by diving into different subjects.

Perusing different sorts widens information and develops a balanced mind.

- **Embrace Skill Development:**

Recognize abilities applicable to individual and expert desires.

Take part in purposeful practice to level up these abilities and remain cutthroat.

- **Network and Seek Mentorship:**

Associate with people who motivate and challenge self-awareness.

Tutors give direction, share bits of knowledge, and add to the persistent turn of events.

- **Attend Workshops and Conferences:**

Take part in occasions that propose active growth opportunities.

Organizing open doors flourish at such social affairs, cultivating development through shared information.

- **Invest in Health and Well-being:**

Physical and mental prosperity structure the establishment for self-improvement.

Standard activity, care rehearses, and satisfactory rest add to by and large imperativeness.

- **Document Your Journey:**

Keep a diary or portfolio to follow individual and expert turns of events.

Thinking about accomplishments and difficulties gives significant bits of knowledge.

- **Financial Literacy:**

Procure information on monetary issues.

Understanding individual accounting records guarantees informed independent direction and long haul security.

- **Challenge Comfort Zones:**

Development happens outside safe places.

Embrace new encounters, go ahead with carefully weighed out courses of action, and welcome difficulties as any open doors for learning.

The Holistic Impact

Investing in oneself isn't bound to scholastic accomplishments; it stretches out to comprehensive prosperity. The expanding influences contact each part of life, making a positive input circle which are recorded underneath:

- **Career Advancement:**
Improved abilities and information push vocation development.

Consistent learning positions people as significant resources in the labor force.

- **Enhanced Creativity:**

A very much supported mind sparkles innovativeness.

Clever thoughts and imaginative arrangements rise up out of a psyche enhanced by different encounters.

- **Emotional Intelligence:**

Self-improvement develops the ability to understand people on a profound level. Solid relational abilities and compassionate comprehension add to enhanced connections.

- **Resilience in Adversity:**

A ceaselessly evolved self climates difficulties with flexibility. Gaining from misfortunes turns into a venturing stone for future achievement.

- **Contributing to Society:**

Proficient and enabled people contribute genuinely to society. An aggregate obligation to self-speculation elevates networks.

BUILDING WEALTH THROUGH SMART MONEY HABITS

To achieve this, developing smart spending habits is essential. Making a financial plan, decreasing costs, keeping away from obligation, mechanizing reserve funds, and contributing shrewdly are probably the most ideal ways to create financial stability. By reliably carrying out these propensities, you can accomplish independence from the rat race and the abundance you want.

How can I save money and build Wealth through smart money habits?

- **Create a Budget:**

Creating a budget is the most important phase in creating shrewd ways of managing money. A spending plan assists you with figuring out your pay and costs and permits you to distribute your cash in a manner that lines up with your monetary objectives.

To make a spending plan, list all your month to month pay sources and costs, including fixed costs like lease or home loan installments, utilities, and vehicle installments, as well as factor costs like food, diversion, and feasting out. When you have your financial plan, audit it consistently to follow your spending and change your portions depending on the situation.

- **Reduce Your Expenses:**

Reducing your expenses is one more basic move toward creating financial stability through savvy ways of managing money. Consider scaling back superfluous costs like eating out, purchasing costly garments or hardware, or taking regular get-aways. All things considered, search for useful cash saving tips for these costs, such as cooking at home, looking for deals, or taking less expensive excursions. By lessening your costs, you can let loose more cash to save and contribute, speeding up your excursion to independence from the rat race.

- **Avoid Debt:**

Obligation can be a critical obstruction to creating financial wellbeing. Interest installments on Mastercards, advances, and different obligations can eat into your investment funds and make it harder to accomplish your monetary objectives.

To keep away from obligation, possibly assume obligation when vital, similar to while purchasing a home or putting resources into your schooling. At the point when you truly do assume obligation, make a point to take care of it as fast as could really be expected, so you can keep away from revenue energizes and free more cash for saving and financial planning.

- **Automate Your Savings:**

Mechanizing your investment funds is another shrewd way of managing money that can assist you with creating financial momentum quicker. Consider setting up a programmed move from your financial records to your bank account every month. Via robotizing your investment funds, you don't need to depend on determination to set aside cash every month, and you can make sure you're reliably putting cash towards your monetary objectives.

- **Invest Wisely:**

Investing is one more basic move toward creating financial momentum through brilliant ways of managing money. Consider putting resources into minimal expense record reserves or other enhanced ventures that line up with your monetary objectives and hazard resistance. By financial planning admirably, you can develop your cash quicker and accomplish your monetary objectives sooner.

ENTREPRENEURIAL SPIRIT: NAVIGATING BUSINESS SUCCESS

An entrepreneurial spirit commonly includes an eagerness to confront difficulties, gain from disappointments, and adjust to changing economic situations, with an emphasis on ceaseless improvement, development, and accomplishing objectives.

Assuming that you're contemplating whether you have a pioneering soul, a few signs are more clear than others. Business visionaries will quite often be daring people who are not effortlessly deflected by disappointment.

They are exceptionally energetic and frequently show an extraordinary enthusiasm for their work. They're not happy with the norm; they're continually searching for new arrangements and state of the art thoughts.

Business people likewise focus on making a move and will quite often be proactive in getting things going. They are proficient at distinguishing potential open doors and tracking down imaginative ways of gaining by them. Assuming that you end up showing these qualities, odds are you have a pioneering soul.

One more significant component is a readiness to learn and adjust as conditions change. Having the option to turn and change your methodology is critical to long haul outcomes in business ventures. Eventually, no one but you can decide whether you have an enterprising soul, yet these are a few normal markers that could be useful to you.

The 5 **P's** of business venture are fundamental characteristics that all entrepreneurs ought to develop to find success;

The first P is **Planning**, which refers to the significance of fostering a reasonable and coordinated technique for accomplishing your objectives. Planning is an important part of making success.

Next is **Passion**, which is the main thrust behind your vision and the inspiration for transforming your fantasies into a reality.

Patience is critical since building a fruitful business takes time and diligence.

The fourth P is **Perseverance**, which is the capacity to remain committed and push through difficulties to make long haul progress.

Finally, **Problem Solving** is the capacity to distinguish and tackle issues imaginatively, which is critical in the continually impacting business world.

By mastering the **5 P's**, business visionaries can fabricate reasonable and effective organizations that endure for the long haul and make them stand apart for more achievement and Riches.

The pioneering soul arises as a directing power, guiding people through the complexities of development, risk-taking, and eventually, achievement. This investigation digs into the substance of enterprising undertakings, revealing the standards and methodologies that make ready for exploring the difficult yet remunerating excursion of business achievement.

Steps to Unleashing The Entrepreneurial Spirit

- **Visionary Ventures:**

Business visionaries imagine potential outcomes where others see difficulties.

Develop a visionary mentality that distinguishes valuable open doors in the midst of intricacies.

- **Risk-Taking Resilience:**

Risk is the heartbeat of business. Embrace carefully thought out plans of action and view disappointments as venturing stones towards development.

- **Innovative Ideation:**

The enterprising soul blossoms with advancement.

Encourage a culture of ceaseless ideation, continuously looking for novel arrangements and approaches.

Foundations of Business Success: Strategies for Entrepreneurs

- **Vital Arranging Accuracy:**

Each effective endeavor starts with a thoroughly examined plan.

Create a vital guide that lines up with business goals.

- **Market Authority:**

Understanding the market is fundamental to progress.

Direct careful statistical surveying to distinguish patterns, needs, and holes.

- **Versatility Munitions stockpile:**

Versatility is the business visionary's most prominent weapon. Remain agile, prepared to turn methodologies in light of market elements.

Exploring Difficulties: Innovative Strategies

- **Monetary Determination:**

Monetary proficiency is a foundation of innovative achievement.

Ace monetary administration to guarantee practical development.

- **Group Strengthening:**

Achievement is definitely not a performance venture; it's a cooperative exertion.

Fabricate and engage in a gifted group that shares the vision and values.

- **Client Driven Approach:**

Consumer loyalty fills business life span.

Focus on client needs, looking for criticism to improve items or administrations.

Moves towards Developing a Versatile Mentality

- **Mindful Leadership:**

Care in authority encourages lucidity and direction. Practice careful authority, remaining present in each enterprising undertaking.

- **Continuous Learning Commitment:**

The innovative excursion is a never-ending expectation to learn and adapt. Develop a promise to continuously get the hang of, keeping up to date with industry patterns.

The Entrepreneurship and Innovation: Catalysts for Success

- **Technological Triumphs:**

Embrace innovation as a push for development. Influence mechanical progressions to smooth out activities and upgrade contributions.

- **Eco-Entrepreneurship:**

Supportability is interwoven with progress.

Coordinate eco-accommodating works on, adjusting business techniques to natural obligation.

Building a Brand Legacy: Entrepreneurial Legacy Beyond Success

- **Brand Building Brilliance:**

A robust brand is an entrepreneur's legacy.

Invest in brand building, crafting a narrative that resonates with the target audience.

- **Community Connection:**

Entrepreneurs are integral community contributors.

Engage in community initiatives, forging connections beyond business transactions.

Championing Ethical Entrepreneurship: Commitment to Integrity

Integrity expects us to be straightforward and honest in all we say and do. Uprightness is apparent through our activities, words, choices and techniques. Our Obligation to Respectability is essential to our business and to the actual center of what our identity is. The following are center moves toward moral business venture:

- **Ethical Decision-Making:**

No Ethical conduct is non-negotiable in entrepreneurship.

Uphold integrity in decision-making, cultivating trust among stakeholders.

- **Social Responsibility in Business:**

Businesses bear a social responsibility like no other.

Integrate socially responsible practices, contributing positively to communities and lives.

Entrepreneurial Wellness: Accomplishment with Individual Prosperity

- **Well-being Wealth:**

Entrepreneurial achievement reaches out past monetary profits. Focus on mental and actual prosperity for supported achievement.

- **Work-Life Integration:**

Balance is the foundation of a satisfying enterprising excursion. Incorporate work and individual life amicably, staying balanced.

THE ART OF NETWORKING: CREATIVE OPPORTUNITIES

Networking is in many cases seen as a conventional trade of merriments in an expert setting, however its quintessence rises above the shallow. At its center, organizing is tied in with building connections that go past quick gains, cultivating associations that endure everyday hardship. Inventive open doors bloom while systems administration changes into a corresponding trade of thoughts, experiences, and backing.

Basically, the more your organization grows, the more individuals know about what you can offer and what you're searching for. Thus, whether you're an entrepreneur or somebody searching for a task, raising your profile can open ways to new business and vocation valuable open doors.

6 Networking Tips for New Entrepreneurs

- Send Individual Recordings.
- Get a Computerized Business Card
- Focus on Others.
- Course in Your People group.
- Put together Your Own Occasions.
- Partake in Gatherings, discussions and Specialty Online Entertainment Locales.

The Power of Authentic Connections

- **Authenticity as a Catalyst:**

Authentic connections form the bedrock of meaningful networking.

Embrace authenticity; let connections be genuine expressions of shared interests and values.

- **Listening as a Skill:**

Listening is an art often overlooked in networking. Cultivate active listening; it's the gateway to understanding needs and identifying collaborative possibilities.

Navigating Networking Platforms: Online and Offline Dynamics

- **Digital Networking:**

The digital era has expanded networking horizons. Master online platforms; leverage social media, professional networks, and forums to broaden your reach.

- **In-Person Impact:**

Face-to-face interactions retain their significance. Attend industry events, seminars, and workshops to create tangible connections that transcend the digital realm.

- **Relationship Building:**

Networking is not transactional; it's relational. Invest time in building relationships; creative opportunities often emerge from the depth of genuine connections.

- **Giving Before Receiving:**

The ethos of networking includes a spirit of generosity. Offer support, insights, and resources without expecting immediate returns.

- **Collaboration Catalyst:**

Networking sets the stage for collaboration. Identify synergies; collaborative ventures often birth creative opportunities beyond individual capacities.

- **Innovative Idea Exchange:**

Diverse networks spark innovation.

Engage with professionals from various fields; the collision of ideas breeds creativity.

The Polished Art of Connection

Timely follow-ups reflect professionalism. After networking events, promptly follow up with an email expressing gratitude and interest.

Networking is a two-way street.
Actively engage in conversations; reciprocate the interest shown by others.

How to Overcome Networking Challenges

- **Introversion and Networking:**

Introverts can excel in networking.
Embrace your strengths; focus on one-on-one interactions and build deeper connections.

- **Networking Fatigue:**

Balance is crucial to prevent networking burnout.

Prioritize quality over quantity; choose events strategically to maintain energy and enthusiasm.

Networking for Personal Growth

- **Mentorship and Guidance:**

Networking extends to mentorship opportunities. Seek guidance from seasoned professionals; mentorship is a conduit for personal and professional growth.

- **Diversity in Connections:**

Diverse networks enrich personal perspectives. Connect with individuals from varied backgrounds; the diversity of thought enhances personal development.

What is a networking opportunity?

Networking opportunities are occasions that permit you to meet and collaborate with new individuals and fabricate associations that might help one or the two players. Organizing makes a common stage that permits you to collaborate with experts, possible clients or merchants in your field.

How To Network When You Hate Networking

- Conduct Your Research Well.
- First Impression is the Last Impression, so make it great.
- Listen More Than You Speak.
- Don't Try To Be Omnipotent of Omniscience.

- Make your Actions Speak Louder Than Words.

OVERCOMING CHALLENGES: RESILIENCE ON THE ROAD TO RICHES

Being resilient means that when we do fall, we rise quickly, we have the solidarity to gain proficiency with the examples we want to learn, and we can leave behind the old to find something new. Generally speaking, flexibility enables us to defeat difficulties, with the goal that we can carry on and with the existence we've generally envisioned.

If you'd like to become more resilient, try some of these tips:

- Get connected. Building strong, healthy relationships with loved ones and friends can give you needed support and help guide you in good and bad times.
- Make every day have meaning.
- Learn from the past.
- Stay hopeful.
- Take care of yourself.
- Take action.

The Nature of Challenges on the Path to Wealth

From economic downturns to personal financial crises, individuals often face challenges that directly impact their monetary well-being.

Resilience in financial planning and adaptability to economic fluctuations are crucial. Career challenges, such as job loss, workplace conflicts, or career transitions, can impede progress.

Resilience involves bouncing back from professional setbacks, learning from experiences, and adapting to new opportunities.

Personal issues, whether health-related, family-oriented, or emotionally taxing, can significantly impact one's pursuit of wealth.

Resilience encompasses the ability to maintain focus and determination despite personal challenges.

Building Resilience: A Foundation for Success

- **Mindset Shift:**

Resilience starts with a change in outlook. Embracing a development mentality that perspectives challenges as any open doors for learning and development is central to beating hindrances.

- **Adaptability:**

Rigidity in the face of difficulties can block progress. Versatility includes exploring vulnerabilities with adaptability and receptiveness to change.

- **Emotional Intelligence:**

Understanding and dealing with feelings, staying cool headed in testing circumstances, and cultivating profound prosperity add to general flexibility.

Case Studies of Resilience in Wealth-Building

- **Entrepreneurial Grit:**

Successful entrepreneurs often face initial failures and setbacks.

Resilience is evident in their ability to learn from failures, pivot when necessary, and persist in the pursuit of their vision.

- **Investment Resilience**:

Financial markets are prone to fluctuations and uncertainties.

Resilient investors weather market volatility, make informed decisions, and stay committed to long-term financial goals.

- **Career Resurgence**:

Individuals who experience career setbacks can bounce back through upskilling, networking, and embracing new opportunities. Resilience propels them to reinvent themselves professionally.

Strategies for Overcoming Challenges

- **Goal Clarity:**

Clearly defined goals serve as beacons during testing times. Strength includes returning to and reaffirming objectives, keeping up with center around the master plan.

- **Continuous Learning:**

A guarantee to deep rooted learning fabricates versatility. Gaining new abilities and information improves flexibility and prepares people to explore advancing difficulties.

- **Support Systems:**

Building and maintaining a network of mentors, advisors, and supportive peers provides invaluable resources during challenging times.

The Role of Failure in Resilience

- **Redefining Failure:**

Failure is an innate piece of the journey to wealth.

Strength includes re-evaluating disappointment and failure as a venturing stone and push to progress, a wellspring of important illustrations and experiences.

- **Learning from Setbacks:**

Always try to learn from your past mistakes or setbacks. Resilience enables individuals to extract lessons from setbacks. Instead of surveying difficulties as detours, resilient people investigate, learn, and use misfortunes as any open doors for development.

Resilience in Wealth Preservation

- **Diversification Strategies:**

Wealth preservation demands resilience against market fluctuations. Diversifying investments and staying informed about economic trends contribute to financial resilience.

- **Adaptive Financial Planning:**

Economic shifts require adaptive financial planning.Resilience is evident in the ability to reassess financial plans, make necessary adjustments, and proactively manage wealth.

The Psychological Aspect of Resilience

- **Positive Psychology:**

Encouraging confidence, appreciation, and an uplifting perspective upgrades versatility even with difficulties.

- **Mindfulness Practices:**

Mindfulness contributes to emotional resilience. Strategies, such as, reflection and care practices, reinforce people's capacity to explore difficulties with a quiet and centered mind.

MINDFULNESS AND WELL BEING: BALANCING SUCCESS AND HAPPINESS

Mindfulness and Care can have many advantages for your balance between serious and fun activities, both temporarily and in the long haul. These can incorporate expanded fulfillment and joy, further developed execution and efficiency, decreased pressure and uneasiness, improved prosperity and wellbeing, and better connections and correspondence.

Making progress toward progress without dismissing individual prosperity, connections, and taking care of oneself can assist with making a more agreeable and fulfilling life. Adjusting the quest for outside objectives with inner satisfaction and appreciation can prompt a more maintainable and real feeling of joy.

The Genuine sorcery happens when achievement and satisfaction are mixed agreeably. Achievement becomes significant when it upgrades a generally blissful life; for the despondent achiever, achievement can feel like a significant weight, pushing them to pursue additional short lived snapshots of happiness.

At its center, care is the craft of being available in the ongoing second. It includes developing an increased consciousness of one's viewpoints, feelings, and the general climate without judgment. This purposeful spotlight on the present works with a more profound association with oneself and the world, offering a significant feeling of lucidity.

Advantages of Mindfulness

- **Stress Reduction:**

Mindfulness serves as a powerful antidote to stress.

By centering attention on the present, individuals can alleviate the burden of future anxieties or past regrets, fostering a calmer and more composed state of mind.

- **Enhanced Well-being:**

The practice of mindfulness contributes to overall well-being.

By nurturing a positive and non-judgmental relationship with oneself, individuals lay the groundwork for a healthier mental and emotional state.

- **Improved Focus and Concentration:**

Mindfulness sharpens focus and concentration.

The ability to anchor one's attention to the current moment aids in enhancing productivity, creativity, and the overall quality of work.

- **Cultivation of Compassion:**

Mindfulness fosters compassion towards oneself and others.

This compassionate perspective forms the basis for nurturing meaningful relationships and building a supportive social network.

- **Emotional Resilience:**

Practicing mindfulness strengthens emotional resilience.

Individuals become better equipped to navigate the ebb and flow of emotions, responding to challenges with equanimity and grace.

Steps to Integrating Mindfulness for Balanced Success and Happiness

- **Begin with Breath Awareness:**

Initiate mindfulness by focusing on the breath. Standard breathing activities such as: careful breathing or profound paunch breathing, ground people right now.

- **Non-judgmental Observation:**

Practice observing thoughts without judgment.

Support a non-basic consciousness of contemplations and sentiments, developing self-acknowledgment and reducing the effect of negative self-talk.

- **Body Scan Meditation:**

Take part in body check reflections to associate with actual sensations.

This training elevates body mindfulness, advancing unwinding and lessening strain.

- **Mindful Activities:**

Infuse mindfulness into daily activities.

Whether it's enjoying a feast, strolling, or doing routine undertakings, connect completely in the experience by pointing out sensations, sights, and sounds.

- **Mindful Listening:**

Improve careful listening abilities.

Effectively tune in without quick reaction, encouraging further associations in private and expert connections.

- **Gratitude Practices:**

Develop appreciation as a foundation of care.

Consistently recognize and value the positive parts of life, ingraining a feeling of happiness.

- **Mindful Movement:**

Integrate careful development into daily practice.

Exercises like yoga or jujitsu incorporate actual development with careful mindfulness, advancing comprehensive prosperity

- **Silent Reflection:**

Cut out minutes for quiet reflection.

Making spaces for calm thought empowers reflection and self-disclosure.

- **Mindful Communication:**

Apply care to correspondence. Focus on clearness, compassion, and non-receptive reactions in discussions, cultivating better and more significant associations.

- **Integrate Mindfulness into Challenges:**

Apply care during testing circumstances. Rather than responding indiscreetly, move toward troubles with a careful outlook, taking into account reactions mindfully.

LEGACY BUILDING: LEAVING A LASTING IMPACT

The definition of a lasting legacy is the positive effect your life has on others, companions, partners, even outsiders.

Your legacy is the amount of the individual qualities, achievements, and activities that reverberate with individuals around you.

Building an enduring legacy is a fundamental part of human life. It envelops the thought of abandoning something significant that will keep on affecting people in the future. Whether it is through our activities, accomplishments, or commitments, the significance of building an enduring legacy couldn't possibly be more significant.

Significance of Legacy Building

- **Perpetuating Values:**

Legacy building allows individuals to pass down core values.

Whether ethical, moral, or philosophical, these values serve as guiding principles for future generations.

- **Influence on Community:**

A well-crafted legacy positively influences the community.

Through philanthropy, community service, or leadership, individuals contribute to the collective well-being, fostering a sense of unity and shared responsibility.

- **Inspiration for Posterity:**

Legacy serves as a source of inspiration for posterity.

Stories of resilience, compassion, and achievement inspire future generations to overcome challenges and strive for greatness.

- **Cultural and Artistic Contributions:**

Legacy building often involves contributions to culture and the arts.

Artists, writers, musicians, and cultural influencers shape society, leaving a lasting impact on how people perceive and experience the world.

- **Educational Empowerment:**

Establishing educational legacies empowers future generations.

Endowing scholarships, founding educational institutions, or advocating for accessible education creates a lasting legacy of knowledge and empowerment.

Steps to Building a Lasting Legacy

- **Define Core Values:**

Clearly define personal and ethical values.

These values act as the foundation upon which a legacy is built, guiding decision-making and actions.

- **Set a Vision:**

Envision the impact one desires to have on the world.

A clear vision serves as a compass, directing efforts toward meaningful contributions.

- **Community Engagement:**

Engage with and contribute to the community.
Acts of service, philanthropy, and community leadership establish a legacy of communal well-being.

- **Document Personal Narratives:**

Preserve personal stories and experiences.
Whether through written memoirs, recorded interviews, or other means, documenting one's journey imparts wisdom to future generations.

- **Cultivate Positive Relationships:**

Foster positive and meaningful relationships.

Building connections based on trust and mutual respect contributes to a legacy of harmonious relationships.

- **Invest in Education:**

Support educational initiatives and opportunities. Empowering others through knowledge ensures a legacy of continuous learning and growth.

- **Environmental Stewardship:**

Advocate for environmental sustainability. Contributing to a healthier planet leaves a legacy of environmental responsibility for the benefit of future generations.

- **Mentorship and Guidance:**

Provide mentorship and guidance to others.

Investing time and knowledge in the development of individuals creates a legacy of mentorship.

- **Create Artistic and Cultural Contributions:**

Contribute to the arts and culture.

Artistic expressions, whether in visual arts, literature, or performance, endure as a cultural legacy.

- **Plan for Succession:**

Develop a plan for succession.

Ensuring that one's work and contributions continue beyond their lifetime is a pivotal aspect of legacy building.

A SUMMARY

As we come closer to concluding this transformative journey towards acquiring a millionaire mindset, it is essential to reflect on the empowering principles that have shaped your mental landscape and power towards having a Millionaire mindset.

The Evolution of Mindset

The journey began with perceiving the force of your viewpoints, the seeds from which your existence blooms. The advancement of attitude included shedding restricting convictions that went about as hindrances to monetary overflow. Embracing the comprehension that your contemplations are latent perceptions as well as dynamic modelers of your world has been a vital disclosure.

Unleashing the Power of Positivity

Positive thinking is not a mere cliché but a catalyst for change. The journey emphasized the cultivation of optimism and the intentional rejection of a scarcity mentality. The adoption of positive affirmations and the reprogramming of your subconscious mind were instrumental in rewiring your mental framework.

Embracing Abundance

Central to the millionaire mindset is the profound shift from scarcity to abundance. This involves acknowledging that the universe is teeming with opportunities waiting to be seized. Abundance isn't merely a financial concept; it's a holistic approach to life, encompassing wealth in relationships, health, and personal growth.

Resilience in the Face of Challenges

The journey uncovered the resilience inherent in a millionaire mindset. Challenges were reframed as opportunities for growth. Rather than succumbing to setbacks, you learned to leverage adversity as a stepping stone toward success. This resilience doesn't eliminate obstacles but transforms your response to them, fostering unwavering determination.

Strategic Goal Setting

Goal setting emerged as a strategic compass, guiding your actions toward tangible success. The journey emphasized not only setting clear and measurable goals but also the importance of breaking them into actionable steps.

This approach ensures that each day becomes a building block in the construction of your envisioned future.

Financial Intelligence and Investment

Your journey delved into the realm of financial intelligence, urging you to become not just an earner but a wise steward of your finances. Investment, both in terms of money and education, became a cornerstone. Understanding the principles of compounding, diversification, and risk management empowered you to navigate the complex landscape of wealth accumulation.

Mastering Time Management

The millionaire mindset recognizes time as an invaluable asset. Strategic time management emerged as a critical component, enabling you to maximize productivity. The journey advocated for the deliberate allocation of time to activities that align with your goals, ensuring that each moment contributes to your overarching success.

Building Wealth Through Smart Money Habits

A millionaire mindset is built on the foundation of smart money habits. The journey explored the significance of budgeting, saving, and mindful spending. By cultivating financial discipline, you not only accumulate wealth but also lay the groundwork for long-term financial security.

Mindfulness and Well-being

The journey emphasized that true wealth extends beyond financial prosperity. Mindfulness and well-being became integral to the millionaire mindset. By balancing success with happiness, you forged a holistic approach to life, recognizing that genuine prosperity encompasses physical, mental, and emotional well-being.

The Power of Visualization

Visualization arose as a strong device in chiseling your world. The excursion investigated the science behind representation, showing how the psyche doesn't recognize genuine and envisioned encounters. Through striking mental symbolism, you tackled the influence to show abundance and success.

Continuous Learning and Adaptation

A millionaire mindset flourishes with consistent learning and variation. The excursion highlighted the significance of keeping up to date with industry patterns, embracing a development outlook, and being available to advancing methodologies. In the always changing scene of progress, the capacity to learn and adjust guarantees supported significance.

CONCLUSION

The excursion to abundance frequently implies going ahead with reasonable plans of action. Millionaires are not speculators, but rather they comprehend the need of getting out of their usual range of familiarity to quickly take advantage of chances. They hold a drawn out vision for their riches, understanding that achievement takes time.

In finishing up your excursion to a Millionaire mentality, it's urgent to perceive that this change is definitely not a limited objective however a long lasting responsibility. The standards investigated are not bound to financial abundance alone; they penetrate each aspect of your reality.

Your contemplations, once bound by constraints, presently take off with conceivable outcomes. Your relationship with time, cash, and achievement has gone through a transformation, mirroring a significant comprehension of your organization in forming your fate.

As you step into the domain of a Millionaire outlook, recall that abundance is a complex gem, transmitting splendor across different elements of your life. Your process isn't simply a quest for wealth; it's an odyssey toward an existence of direction, satisfaction, and enduring effect.

The millionaire mentality isn't characterized by the equilibrium in your financial balance alone, but by the extravagance you bring to your connections, the positive effect you make locally, and the heritage you create for people in the future.

Thus, as you set out on the extensive skyline enlightened by your recently procured attitude, convey with you the insight acquired from this excursion. Your true capacity for thriving is endless, and the millionaire outlook is definitely not a far off desire, it's a condition of being that penetrates each thought, activity, and choice.

May your excursion to a Millionaire mentality be the force for an existence of overflow, satisfaction, and getting through progress. As you explore the strange waters of your future, may the standards you've embraced guide you higher than ever of accomplishment, making history.

Congrats on arriving at the perfection of your extraordinary excursion, may your millionaire outlook be the compass that drives you to a future loaded up with boundless conceivable outcomes, valuable open doors, influence, abundance and wealth.

www.ingramcontent.com/pod-product-compliance
Lightning Source LLC
Chambersburg PA
CBHW071207290526
45796CB00008B/176